Rhyming Alphabet

by Ron Benson

Illustrated by Laurie Stein

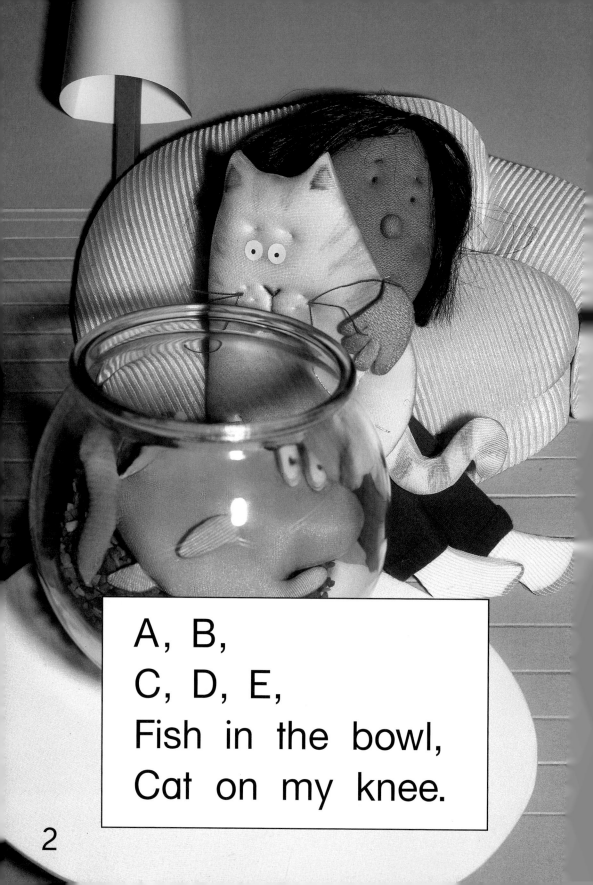

A, B,
C, D, E,
Fish in the bowl,
Cat on my knee.

2

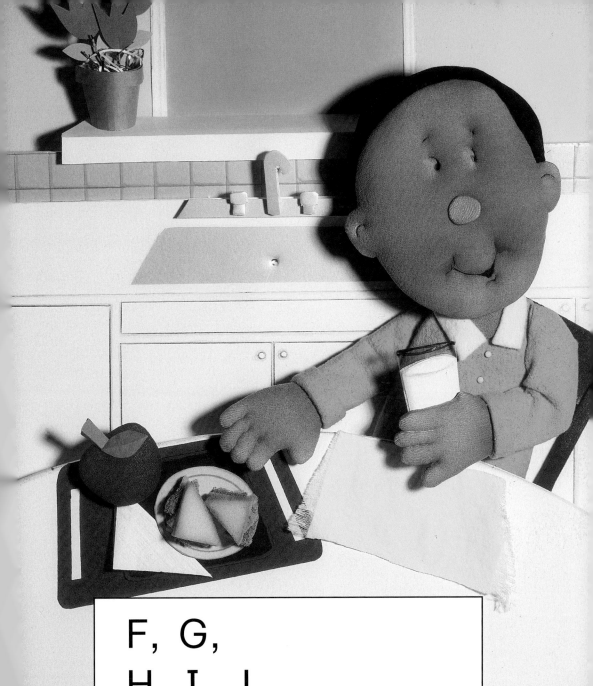

F, G,
H, I, J,
Milk in the glass,
Food on a tray.

K, L,
M, N, O,
Toys on the shelf,
Books in a row.

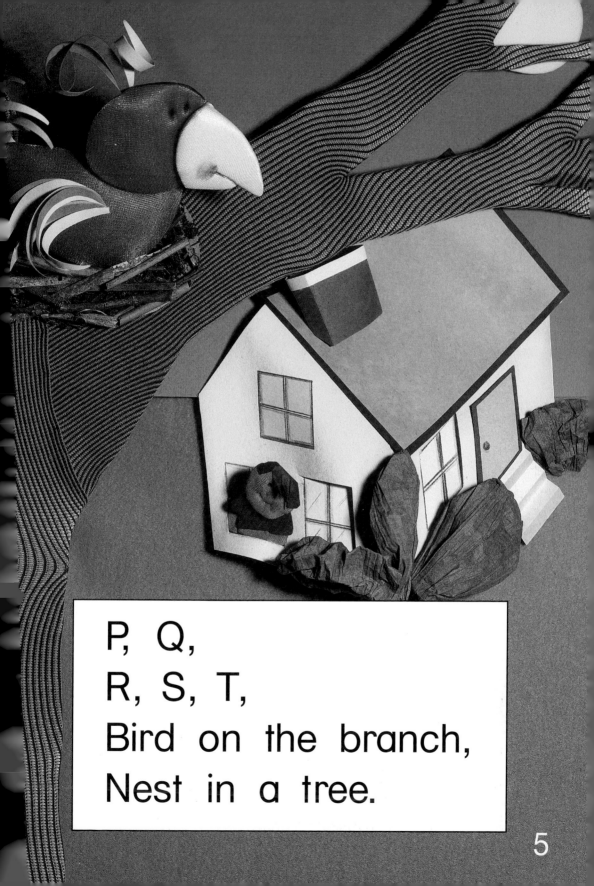

P, Q,
R, S, T,
Bird on the branch,
Nest in a tree.

5

U, V,
W, X, Y,
Worm on the ground,
Moon in the sky.

Z, Z,
Z, Z, Z,
Nighttime is here.
Jump into bed!

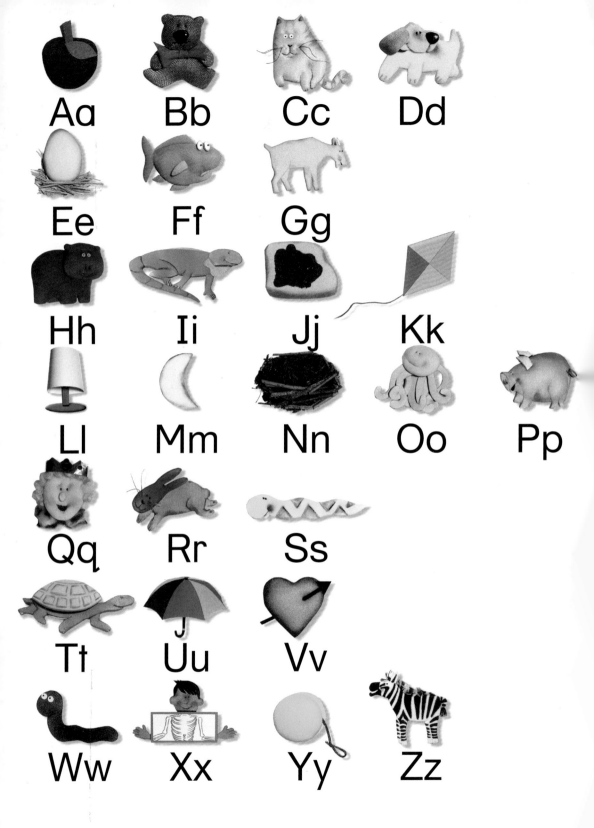

Aa   Bb   Cc   Dd

Ee   Ff   Gg

Hh   Ii   Jj   Kk

Ll   Mm   Nn   Oo   Pp

Qq   Rr   Ss

Tt   Uu   Vv

Ww   Xx   Yy   Zz